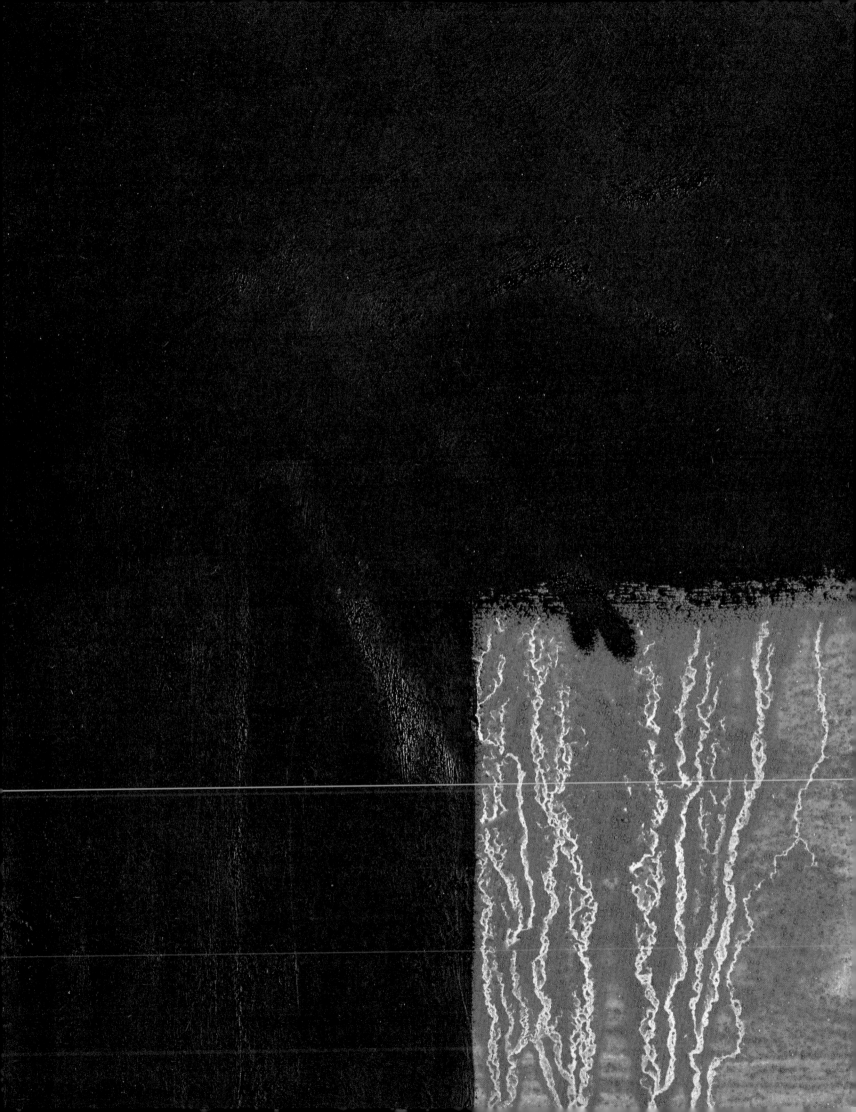

A layer in the kiln

Preceding page: Dry figures outside Don Isaac's kiln
Opposite page: Matías loading pieces

Steam rising from Don Marcelino's kiln: the first firing

The opened kiln

FIELD

Installation at the Old City Jail, Charleston

Bed (1981)

Three Ways (1981–1982)

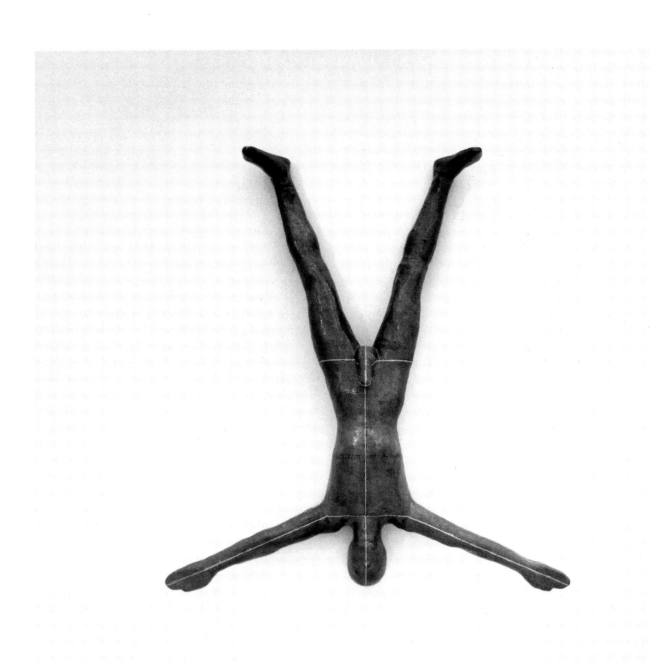

As Above, So Below (1988)

grid also calls forth the overlay of cultural methods of categorization and analysis on the indefinite continuum of life-forces. Here again is the tragic inner polarity. Universal in its life-force and its hope for the future, the figure is bound finitely to a perilous conditionality that can destroy its universality along with its body.

In a stillness that reflects meditational experience, the figures sit, stand, crouch, lie down, bend over, walk. Yet in the midst of these real-life functions, they bear various stamps of an Orphic or metaphysical otherness. Some (for example, *Three Ways*, 1981) are pierced with holes at their highest points – escape openings for an upward flow of energy impelled by a destructive transcendence to leave the body behind. One (*As Above, So Below*, 1988) is spread-eagled as in the astronomical mandalas of the Renaissance, crucified, as it were, on the intersection of the universal and the particular, as he floats upside down above the floor.

In other cases, the arrangement of figures, or their placement in natural locations, involves theatrical implications portending the apocalypse as a theatre of black, burning loneliness. In one classic photograph, the three figures of *Land, Sea and Air II*, 1982, stand, lie or crouch on the beach of the ocean like last lonely remnants of a dream of human life that the tide of a cyclical destruction is about to erase. They seem engrossed in bare attention to what is happening, or about to happen, to them, offering their awareness as the only power they have in the face of an overwhelming desolation and abandonment.

For Gormley (as for some other recent artists), art in general and sculpture in particular – with its special claim to nonillusionistic reality – is potentially an evolutionary tool, reflecting the Jungian (and Teilhardian) model of evolution as a process that moves from matter to mind. *Mind*, 1984, articulates the challenge of necessary changes in consciousness as the imbalance of the dual nature threatens to go out of control. A leaden cloud like a giant brain is affixed to the ceiling as if floating to the highest available level, expressing the contradictory themes of upward impulse and downward gravity, the transformative power of the human brain along with its inert physicality. It has within it both the need to float above in a realm

Land, Sea and Air II (1982)

Out of this World (1983–1984)

Mind (1984)

of universals and the entrapment in the body that counters transcendence with destruction.[2]

By the mid-1980s, Gormley began to focus on the idea of a mind-generated rebirth, and this motif in turn led to a second essential material, terra-cotta, which has since gradually taken over, displacing the inorganic lead. With connotations of prime matter or primeval mud, terra-cotta recalls the potter's clay out of which, in an ancient theological metaphor, the creating deity fashioned the first beings, as in the Akkadian creation epic and elsewhere. A motif repeated in a number of works is the emergence of a smaller figure or object from a larger one, usually from the head, as in *The Beginning, the Middle, the End, Out of This World*, 1983–1984, and *Idea*, 1985. The small emerging figure, of terra-cotta, seems a metal excrescence or dream creation of the larger lead figure. It is the dream of the future about to emerge from the fact of the present. Again, it is consciousness emerging from matter after the long ordeal of its alchemical purification.

Idea (1985)

The Beginning, the Middle, the End (1983–1984)

In *Man Asleep*, 1985, several dozen terra-cotta homunculi walk past the head of a leaden male figure that seems to be lying asleep. As a suggestion of dreamed selves setting out from the sleeping brain, the work might be associated with the Hindu sculptural icon of Vishnu Anantasayin, in which the god lies asleep upon the ocean and dreams the world, which emerges from his sleeping mind. As such it has as much to do with the threatened end of the world of form as with a new beginning; into the oceanic abyss underlying the sleeping god's dream, countless worlds and beings have been reabsorbed at the time of the *nigredo*. Gormley has also thought of it as Adam's sleep from which Eve was produced and, through her, the stream of the humanity of the future. *Man Asleep* is the principal forerunner of *Field*, from which the leaden figure is finally altogether absent, and the terra-cotta figurines produced somehow as forms of its consciousness occupy the whole field of the future.

Field represents a radical change in Gormley's work, in its reduction in scale of the figures, elimination of the artist's body and the element of lead from the process, and vast proliferation of figures. The terra-cotta figurines, seemingly connected with the primacy of consciousness and hence associated with a hopeful prognostication of the future, represent a new era of feeling. The half-formed tiny beings never challenge the legitimacy of the leaden giants they are replacing but offer themselves to the world with a greater intimacy and warmth. *Field* is a place of feeling, a place for the feeling of the future.

Gormley has made three versions of *Field* from 1989 to 1993. The number of terra-cotta figures has dramatically increased from one hundred and fifty in the first version to forty thousand in the present one. In this work, the earlier lead figures are tacitly replaced by the consciousness of the viewer, who, excluded from the clay figures' space and their company, is nevertheless summoned by them. They constitute a kind of seedbed, or place of becoming, whose fulfilment is the responsibility of the viewer.

The current version of *Field* involved a collaboration that was a constituent element of the work – not merely of its physical presence but of its meaning: it arose

Field I (1989)

Field II (1989)

through a co-operative engagement with Third World humanity, to whom the future, according to current demographic projections, belongs. Gormley worked on these thousands of terra-cotta figurines with the Texca family of brickmakers in Cholula, Mexico. Each small, rudimentary figure, from seven to twenty-two centimetres tall, was handmade, sun-dried and then baked in a brick kiln. Gormley was intrigued by the fact that this family of rural artisans, who work out-of-doors in an agricultural manner, mass-produce a standardized urban product for the nearby metropolis of Mexico City. For the first time in a career that has involved various collaborations, Gormley turned the most intimate and meaningful parts of production over to the hands of his collaborators. In previous versions, he had insisted on making the head and eyes – the seats and expressions of consciousness – himself; in this case, each artisan made his or her own figures completely. The work became a reservoir of feeling into which many related personalities poured their vibrations through their hands. The subject, the material and the process of production were thus interlinked in their human implications.

In the 1991 installation at the Salvatore Ala Gallery in New York, the viewer first encountered empty space and then, after wandering quizzically through an empty room, found in the large room at the back the overwhelming mass of small figures, all gazing up through their hollow black eye sockets and arrayed on the floor like an irregular tide. Like late Neolithic and early Bronze Age figurines from Mesopotamia, the Indus Valley and elsewhere, they have an infantile innocence and vulnerability in their rudimentary, barely formed bodies. Seemingly awaiting some call, they mass in intense upward gazing, as if pleading for honourable survival. Facing them, the viewer may become aware of the oblivion of a future that will arise from, and yet replace, his or her body, while at the same time recognizing a responsibility towards the future, which will inhabit the world that the humanity of the present makes for it. Their look of mute expectation and restrained beseeching reminds us of our role as custodians of the earth and preparators of its destiny.

Gormley's oeuvre stems from direct experience and does not involve the Modern-